RICHARD TULLOCH is one of Australia's leading writers of plays, screenplays and books for young audiences. His more than fifty plays include *Hansel and Gretel ... A Tale of Our Times*, *The Happy Prince*, *Carnival of the Animals*, *Stella and the Moon Man*, *Lulie the Iceberg* (all for Theatre of Image), *Year 9 are Animals*, *Hating Alison Ashley* and *Twinkle, Twinkle Little Fish* (a Sydney Festival production that also played on Broadway in New York). His plays have earned him four Australian Writers' Guild AWGIE Awards. He has performed his one-man storytelling show *Storyman* thousands of times in theatres, schools and libraries around the world. He has written over 150 episodes of *Bananas in Pyjamas* and contributed scripts to numerous other television series. He has had over 35 children's books published, including *Stories from Our House*, *Danny in the Toybox*, *Beastly Tales*, *Twisted Tales* and the very popular *Weird Stuff* novels. His screenplay for the animated film *Ferngully II – The Magical Rescue* was nominated for Best Script at the US Annie Awards in 1998. He also now works as a travel writer, regularly published in the *Sun-Herald* newspaper and on his blog.

THE BOOK OF EVERYTHING

The play

Adapted by Richard Tulloch

From the novel by Guus Kuijer

CURRENCY PRESS
The performing arts publisher

CURRENCY PLAYS

First published in 2009
by Currency Press Pty Ltd,
PO Box 2287, Strawberry Hills, NSW, 2012, Australia
enquiries@currency.com.au
www.currency.com.au

in association with Company B Belvoir, Sydney.

This revised edition published in 2011.

Reprinted in 2012 (twice), 2013, 2014, 2015, 2017, 2019, 2021.

The Book of Everything, the play copyright © Richard Tulloch, 2009;
illustrations within the text copyright © Kim Carpenter, 2009

Cataloguing-in-publication data for this title is available from the National
Library of Australia website: www.nla.gov.au

Typeset by Dean Nottle for Currency Press.
Cover design by Tim Kliendienst.
Front cover shows Matthew Whittet.

Currency Press acknowledges the Traditional Owners of the Country on which
we live and work. We pay our respects to all Aboriginal and Torres Strait
Islander Elders, past and present.

Contents

THE BOOK OF EVERYTHING

    Act One   1

    Act Two   27

WRITER'S NOTE

I now count myself lucky to live in Amsterdam, my wife's home town, for about half of each year. I love its beauty and culture, work at learning its language and admire its long history of openness and tolerance. Shame about the weather, but you can't have everything.

I was there when Kim Carpenter, Artistic Director of Theatre of Image, emailed me and asked if I knew anything about a writer called Guus Kuijer. Kim had just read *The Book of Everything*, and loved it. Of course I knew about Guus Kuijer; he's won many Dutch literature awards, and in the Netherlands, he's familiar to everyone who has been a child since his first books about a girl called Madelief appeared in the 1970s.

When I read *The Book of Everything*, I loved it too. It is remarkable how a slim book can say so much about the difficult topics of facing fear and violence, finding strength and happiness, and questioning religious beliefs. These themes may not be the usual stuff of children's entertainment, but Kuijer never shies away from complexity. Like all the best writers for young people, he trusts them to do some thinking.

In *The Book of Everything*, Kuijer tells a story from the time of his childhood, set in Amsterdam as the city emerged fro the trauma of German occupation during World War II. Amsterdam was spared the bombing which destroyed central Rotterdam, and missed the heavy fighting which left towns like Arnhem in ruins. But most of Amsterdam's large Jewish population was deported to concentration camps, while others went into hiding. Anne Frank is the most famous of these. Her family and thousands like them depended on the bravery of ordinary Dutch people like Mrs van Amersfoort in this story. I don't know the details of Kuijer's childhood, but I do know that he was born during the war, grew up in a religious family and that, like Thomas, he gradually came to question the ethics of stories in the Bible. For instance, was it fair for God to punish all the Egyptians for something their pharaoh did wrong? If God really was an all-powerful and loving father, why did he let his son Jesus be crucified? Children do think about these things. As a child I loved animals, and wondered why God drowned most of them and only saved a few on Noah's Ark.

If it is appropriate to tell children these stories, and I'm sure it is, we should encourage them to consider when and why they were written, to question how they relate to their own lives and to form their own opinions about their meaning.

Melbourne writer John Nieuwenhuizen's excellent English translation of the novel *The Book of Everything* has been much acclaimed, but for this stage adaptation I worked from the Dutch original. I have tried to remain true to Kuijer's powerful story and elegant language, but there will be differences between the play and the novel. I hope you will want to read both.

I am very grateful to Guus Kuijer for trusting me to do a faithful adaptation, to Kim Carpenter's Theatre of Image and Company B Belvoir for commissioning the script and mounting the production, and to the cast and crew, both of this production and of a creative development workshop in 2008, who generously contributed their ideas to the final draft.

*I can't remember that God was ever a topic of conversation
for us children. I mean in the street when there were no
adults around. That is remarkable, when you consider that
our lives were saturated with God ... But in the street, that
whole pious world disappeared over the horizon. We were
cowboys and Indians, Ivanhoe and Robin Hood, cops and
robbers, but never Jesus.*

*My father heartily looked forward to the second coming,
and prayed regularly and fervently, "Come Lord Jesus,
come soon!" And I remember that as a child I thought,
"Yes, but not until after my birthday."*

*I can't remember any child who saw anything in the
afterlife, because to look forward to that is to look down on
the life that we have here on earth. Our prayer was always
"Stay where you are Lord, and don't move!" Children love
life, you know, and so they should.*

— Guus Kuijer

SCRIPT DEVELOPMENT

This stage adaptation was commissioned by Kim Carpenter's Theatre of Image.

The script was further developed in a workshop in 2008 under the direction of Neil Armfield, with designer Kim Carpenter, composer Iain Grandage and actors Sacha Horler, Deborah Kennedy, Russell Kiefel, Odile le Clezio, Rebecca Massey, Kate Mulvany, Matthew Whittet and Dan Wyllie.

The cast and crew of the first production also contributed to this script. Thank you all for your enthusiasm, generosity and valuable input.

This adaptation of *The Book of Everything* was first produced by
Company B Belvoir and Kim Carpenter's Theatre of Image at Belvoir
St Upstairs Theatre, Sydney, on 2 January 2010, with the following cast:

MARGOT	Alison Bell
FATHER / BUMBITER	Peter Carroll
MRS VAN AMERSFOORT	Julie Forsyth
MUSICIAN	Iain Grandage
MOTHER	Claire Jones
AUNTY PIE	Deborah Kennedy
JESUS	John Leary
ELIZA	Yael Stone
THOMAS	Matthew Whittet

Director, Neil Armfield
Set & Costume Designer, Kim Carpenter
Composer, Iain Grandage
Lighting Designer, Nigel Levings
Choreographer, Julia Cotton
Sound Designer, Steve Francis
Assistant Director, Eamon Flack
Stage Manager, Mark Lowrey
Assistant Stage Manager, Sophie Baker

CHARACTERS

THOMAS KLOPPER, aged 9, nearly 10
MARGOT KLOPPER, aged 16
ELIZA WITH THE LEATHER LEG, aged 16
MOTHER
FATHER
BUMBITER
MRS VAN AMERSFOORT
AUNTIE PIE
JESUS

And also:

CHILDREN, CHURCH CONGREGATION, READING OUT LOUD CLUB
GUESTS

SETTING

Amsterdam, summer, 1951.

The house of the Klopper family in the 'Old South' area of the city. It is a middle-class area with rows of red brick apartments. The apartment is austere, with little decoration other than a tropical fish tank and a painting of Jesus.

Next door is the apartment of Mrs van Amersfoort, lined with books and cluttered with magical knick-knacks.

Other locations are the streets of Amsterdam and a church service house.

STYLE

This is an ensemble piece; actors not involved in particular scenes sometimes remain on stage, observing, commenting on the action and supplying sound effects and props as required.

Kim Carpenter's design for the original production featured a large copy of Thomas's book, *The Book of Everything*, standing upstage centre. Pages were turned during the performance to reveal naively painted representations of each of the different locations.

ACT ONE

PROLOGUE

Cheerful music, suggesting a Dutch street organ.

THOMAS *sits by a window, writing on the cover of a new exercise book.*

THOMAS: *The Book of Everything,* by Thomas Klopper, aged nine... [*crossing it out and writing again*] nearly ten. Address: Breughelstreet 3, Amsterdam, Holland, Europe, Northern Hemisphere, Earth, Solar System, Galaxy, Universe, Space. Year: 1951.

Cheerful music.

My family. There are four people in my family. Me, Thomas Klopper, aged nearly ten, Pappa, who is my father. His name is Mr Abel Klopper.

FATHER *enters the acting area, strides stiffly across it and leaves.*

My mother is called Mamma, Mrs Klopper and Jannie. She is very kind to everybody.

MOTHER *crosses the stage, pausing to give a small present to someone in the audience.*

My sister is Margot and she is sixteen.

MARGOT *flounces across the acting area.*

Margot is stupid.

MARGOT *stops and turns on* THOMAS, *threatening him, then exits.*

My neighbours.

AUNTIE PIE *wobbles on, riding a bicycle.*

Auntie Pie always rides a bike, even in the rain. She has been riding for forty-eight years, but she is not very good at it.

AUNTIE PIE *and her bike wobble off. The sound of a crash offstage.*

Next door to us lives a witch. Her name is Mrs van Amersfoort and she always wears black dresses.

MRS VAN AMERSFOORT crosses. She is dressed in black and a little eccentric, muttering to herself as she walks.

Mrs van Amersfoort gets teased a lot, because she is a witch.

Two children enter and start teasing her, walking behind her and imitating her gait. MRS VAN AMERSFOORT exits too.

The scariest thing in our neighbourhood is the Bumbiter.

The BUMBITER, a large vicious dog, springs into the acting area.

He's a dog that dashes down our street, big and wild and mean. Nobody knows where he comes from—he's just there. And he bites you on the bottom!

The BUMBITER, played by the actor playing FATHER, runs around snarling, trying to bite the bottoms of the children, played by the rest of the cast. They scatter in terror, hands covering their backsides.

The BUMBITER snarls, lost and alone in the space, then he too exits.

SCENE ONE

THOMAS: [*to the audience*] I don't know why, but I see things that nobody else can see. I write them all down in my book, *The Book of Everything*. Like today, when I saw a terrible hailstorm in Jan van Eyckstreet. In the middle of summer!

There is a crash of thunder and a violent hailstorm starts.

Watching actors make the storm with a series of hand slaps, a gathering crescendo alarming THOMAS.

Mamma! Mamma!

He puts his hands over his ears. He runs home as MOTHER enters.

MOTHER: What is it, Thomas?
THOMAS: Winter's here!
MOTHER: Really? How did you get that idea?
THOMAS: I saw it, a big hailstorm. The leaves were blasted off the trees.
MOTHER: Thomas, look—the trees are all still green.
THOMAS: The trees here are green. But round the corner in the Jan van Eyckstreet all the leaves have been ripped off. The whole street is covered in them!

MOTHER *is a little concerned.*

MOTHER: If you say so, Thomas.

She ruffles his hair and leaves.

THOMAS: Mamma doesn't believe I saw it, but I know I did! Now, where was I? [*He writes in his book again.*] My favourite colour is blue. My favourite food is apple tart. My favourite animals are guppies, which are fish…es. When I grow up, I'm going to be a…

FATHER *enters.*

FATHER: I'm home.

FATHER *is home from the office. He sets down his briefcase and removes his coat, hanging it on a coat hanger. Everything he does is precise, following a stiff, strict routine.*

MOTHER *quickly scurries to set a place at the table for him.*

MOTHER: Thomas, Margot, Pappa's home!

THOMAS: I still don't know what my book's going to be about.

FATHER *sits at the dining table.*

MARGOT *passes, on her way to the living room.*

MARGOT: [*imitating* MOTHER] Thomas, Margot, Pappa's home!

THOMAS: What are books about, Margot?

She won't allow herself to get into a philosophical discussion with him.

MARGOT: Thomas—you're such a nine-year-old!

THOMAS: Nearly ten.

MARGOT: You can't even read long words.

THOMAS: I love long words, especially if I don't know what they mean.

MARGOT: Yes, like 'ignoramus'!

THOMAS: You think just because you're my big sister, you know every-thing. Just because you're sixteen you think you're a genius! You are so dumb, Margot!

MARGOT: Dutch language—nine, Maths—ten, English—eight, Geog-raphy—nine, History—ten.

THOMAS: [*to the audience*] It's amazing that Margot can get good school reports and still be as dumb as an onion!

They move towards the dining table.

MARGOT: Anyway, all the really good books are about love, and you're too young to know about things like that.

They sit at the table as FATHER *says grace.*

FATHER: Bless us, O Lord, and these Thy gifts, which of Thy bounty we are about to receive. Amen. [*He sets a Bible firmly on the table.*] All the important books are about God. All the important stories are here in the Bible.

MOTHER: [*trying to keep the peace*] Books can be about love and God.

But FATHER *must have the last word.*

FATHER: Oh? Who reads the books in this house, you or me?

MOTHER: You do.

FATHER: So who knows about books?

MOTHER: [*meekly*] You do.

FATHER: Then I'll thank you not to contradict me when you don't know what you're talking about.

There is a tense silence. MARGOT *stifles a giggle.*

THOMAS: It hailed really hard in the Jan van Eyckstreet today, Pappa. The leaves were blasted right off the trees.

MOTHER *reaches out to him.*

FATHER: It's a sin to tell lies, Thomas. 'Keep thy tongue from evil and thy lips from speaking guile.' Psalm 34.

THOMAS: But I saw it, I really—

FATHER: Thomas!

THOMAS: Sorry, Pappa.

MARGOT: Psychologically defective.

MOTHER: Thomas is alright.

All eat in awkward silence.

FATHER *takes the Bible.*

FATHER: Today we are reading from the Book of Exodus, chapter five. [*Reading*] Moses and Aaron went in, and told Pharaoh, Thus saith the Lord God of Israel, Let my people go, that they may hold a feast unto me in the wilderness. And Pharaoh said, Who is the Lord, that I should obey his voice to let Israel go? I know not the Lord, neither will I let Israel go.

As he reads, THOMAS*'s attention wanders. He distracts himself (and the audience!) by playing games with his bowl and cutlery.* FATHER *closes the Bible.*

Tomorrow we shall read further, about how God punished the pharaoh for disobeying His will.

> MOTHER *hustles* THOMAS *out of the room.*

MOTHER: Bedtime, Thomas.

> *She ruffles* THOMAS*'s hair.*

You do have some funny stuff in there, don't you, my little dreamer? Sometimes I wonder what's going on with you.

THOMAS: Do you think I'm a little bit nice, Mamma?

MOTHER: I think you're very, very, very, very 'a little bit nice'! You're the sweetest boy in the whole world.

> *She hugs him, trying to hide her tears, then leaves him.*

THOMAS: I hate it when Mamma is sad. [*He writes in the book again.*] When I grow up, I'm going to be... happy.

SCENE TWO

Church bells ring.

THOMAS *and* MARGOT *walk in the street.* MARGOT *wears a headscarf covering her hair.*

JESUS ACTOR: That summer in Amsterdam it was boiling hot for a whole week.

AUNTIE PIE ACTOR: So hot that bicycle tyres melted on the bitumen.

> THOMAS *spots something in the (imaginary) canal and dawdles to examine it.*

THOMAS: So hot that tropical fish were swimming in the canal. I saw them with my own eyes. Dozens of them. They were guppies, like the ones in our fish tank at home. But nobody would believe that I saw them in the canal. Hey, look Margot—guppies!

MARGOT: Thomas, we don't have time for these aquatic apparitions!

> ELIZA *enters. She has a 'leather leg', an artificial limb that creaks as she walks. She carries a beach towel, and waves to* MARGOT, *a school friend.*

ELIZA: Hey, Margot!

MARGOT: Hi, Eliza. Where are you going?

ELIZA: Where else on a hot Sunday? Zandvoort Beach. How about you?

MARGOT: [*indicating her headscarf*] We're walking to church.

ELIZA: Oh. Which church do you go to?

MARGOT: It's not even a real church. We go to someone's house in Amsterdam West. Pappa's leading the service today. You wouldn't believe how boring it is. [*Calling*] Thomas!

ELIZA: You're walking to Amsterdam West in this heat? Why don't you catch the tram?

MARGOT: [*with irony*] God wouldn't like it. God doesn't want the trams to run on Sundays.

ELIZA: God doesn't like trams?

MARGOT: Not on Sundays, that's what Pappa says. Apparently, the two worst things in the world are being a traitor in the War, and riding in a tram on Sunday. [*Calling*] Thomas!

> THOMAS *leaves the canal and runs to catch up with* MARGOT.

THOMAS: They're swimming in the canal, Margot. I can see them! Fantail guppies and spike swordtails and—

> *He stops short when he sees* ELIZA.

ELIZA: Who's this?

MARGOT: It's my brother Thomas. Ignore him. He suffers from infantile hallucinations.

ELIZA: Hello, Thomas. I'm Eliza.

> *It is a magic moment.*

> THOMAS *is smitten, and unable to meet* ELIZA*'s eye. But dropping his gaze means he's looking at her leg.*

MARGOT: It's rude to stare at people, Thomas! Don't you know anything?

ELIZA: It's fine, Margot. I'm used to it. See, Thomas, it's just my leather leg. It creaks when I walk. [*She creaks around on it, jokingly using it to squeak out a little rhythm.*] You want to touch it?

> *She offers it to him.* THOMAS *reaches out to touch it, but when he gets closer he is too shy and withdraws his hand.*

THOMAS: No, thank you.

ELIZA: What were you looking at over there?

THOMAS: Tropical fish, in the canal. Guppies.

ELIZA: Where?

> MARGOT *can't believe* ELIZA *is paying attention to him.*

MARGOT: Eliza, he's nine.

> *But* ELIZA *joins* THOMAS *staring into the canal.*

ELIZA: Oh, yes—there they are! People flush them down the toilet when they go on holidays. Did you know there are crocodiles living in the sewers too?

THOMAS: Really? Have you seen them?

ELIZA: Just a little one, swimming in our toilet. Only this big. [*She holds up her little finger—the only one on her deformed hand. Then seeing* THOMAS *staring at it*] Yeah, I've got a funny hand too, haven't I? Hey, that's my tram! 'Bye, Margo. 'Bye, Thomas. Wait for me, driver—can't you see I'm a cripple?

> *She runs off, obviously hobbling, but clearly not embarrassed in the slightest.*

THOMAS: [*to the audience*] I felt a sort of electric shock in my stomach. Eliza was so… beautiful. And she understood what I saw.

MARGOT: If you make us late for church, Thomas, Pappa will kill you. Then I'll kill you too.

THOMAS: What happened to Eliza's fingers?

MARGOT: Shut up!

> *They exit.*

SCENE THREE

Music continues quietly as THOMAS *and* MARGOT *hurry to join* MOTHER *and* FATHER *as they arrange seating for a church service and greet other parishioners, including* AUNTIE PIE.

FATHER: The Lord be with you, Pie [*pronounced 'Pee'*].

AUNTIE PIE: And with you, Abel. [*To* THOMAS] Hello, my little sausage—everything tickety-boo?

> *She kisses* MARGOT *and* THOMAS.

THOMAS & MARGOT: [*together*] Hello, Auntie Pie.

AUNTIE PIE: Phew, is it hot enough for you or what?

FATHER *greets other parishioners.*

FATHER: The Lord be with you… The Lord be with you… The Lord be with you…

THOMAS: Sunday is a day you have to push in front of you like a wheelbarrow. Other days just roll off the bridge by themselves. On Sunday we aren't allowed to play games, or ride on a tram, or whistle.

A bird calls. THOMAS *looks up at it.*

Only birds can whistle, because they don't know it's Sunday. Birds don't have souls.

FATHER *stands at the front, leading the service.*

FATHER: Hear the word of the Lord as it is written in the Book of Exodus, chapter nine. 'And the Lord said unto Moses and unto Aaron, Take to you handfuls of ashes of the furnace, and let Moses sprinkle it toward the heaven in the sight of the Pharaoh…'

His voice drones on with the reading as THOMAS *looks around the congregation.*

THOMAS: [*to the audience*] Not many people come to our church. They're mostly old or blind or deaf or lame, with warts on their chins.

FATHER: 'And it shall become small dust in all the land of Egypt, and shall be a boil breaking forth with blains upon man, and upon beast, and upon all the land of Egypt…'

THOMAS: [*to the audience*] There are only two other children at our church. Two sisters who are so pale they're not going to last much longer. I give them till 1955.

FATHER: 'And the magicians could not stand before Moses because of the boils, for the boil was upon the magicians, and upon all the Egyptians.'

THOMAS: That's a lot of boils!

MOTHER *directs* THOMAS*'s attention to* FATHER.

FATHER: I want to think today about the true meaning of those plagues of Egypt. God sent the plagues of Egypt to punish the pharaoh for his wickedness. But those plagues were also a warning to the people of Egypt; the same warning that God sends to us here right now—that a time will come when those that do wrong will have to answer for their sins.

ALL: [*singing*]
>   Lord, we like sheep have gone astray
>   And wandered in the cold,
>   O guide us with Thy mighty hand
>   And lead us to Thy fold.

A hummed second verse of the hymn continues under the following.

MARGOT: [*to the audience*] Sunday church service was long…

AUNTIE PIE: [*to the audience*] And the seats were hard.

>   THOMAS *looks around the congregation.* MOTHER *adjusts* MARGOT*'s scarf so it covers her hair.*

THOMAS: [*to the audience*] Ladies have to cover their heads when they go to church. You aren't allowed to see their hairdos. It's alright for men—they don't have hairdos.

>   *The hymn ends.*

FATHER: [*singing*]
>   Almighty God,
>   You see into the uttermost depths of our hearts.

PARISHIONERS: [*singing*]
>   Lord God, have mercy on us miserable sinners,
>   And forgive us our transgressions.

FATHER: [*singing*]
>   You know that we are unworthy.

>   *He nods to* MOTHER *who responds, singing alone.*

MOTHER: [*singing*]
>   Lord God, have mercy on us miserable sinners,
>   And forgive us our transgressions.

FATHER: [*singing*]
>   We have sinned against you in thought, word and deed.

>   *He nods to another parishioner,* AUNTIE PIE, *who responds.*

AUNTIE PIE: [*singing*]
>   Lord God, have mercy on us miserable sinners,
>   And forgive us our transgressions.

FATHER: [*singing*]
>   We are not worthy to be called your children.

He nods to THOMAS.

THOMAS: [*singing*]
   Lord God, have mercy on us miserable singers,
   And forgive us our tram sessions.

  The organ music cuts out abruptly and there is a deathly silence.
  MARGOT *giggles.* FATHER *silences her with a look that could kill.*

THOMAS: What?

  Organ music blares again. The parishioners file out of church,
  clearing the church seats as they go.

SCENE FOUR

The family walk into their house, FATHER *striding in front.*

AUNTIE PIE ACTOR: As they walked home, Thomas saw that his father
  was angry about something.

  THOMAS *attempts to break the tension with some light chatter.*

THOMAS: I saw guppies today, Pappa. They were swimming in the canal.

  FATHER *pointedly ignores him.*

JESUS ACTOR: The house was as silent as the grave.
ELIZA ACTOR: Two sparrows on the windowsill blew on shrill trumpets.
JESUS ACTOR: They didn't know it was Sunday.

  The family sits.

FATHER: Thomas, stand up.
THOMAS: Stand up?
FATHER: Stand!
MOTHER: Why?
FATHER: Because I say so.
MARGOT: [*with heavy sarcasm*] That's why.

  THOMAS *stands.*

FATHER: Would you repeat what you sang during the responses?

  THOMAS *looks at* MOTHER, *uncertain.*

 Look at me and sing!
THOMAS: [*singing tentatively*]
   Lord God have mercy on us miserable singers...
   And forgive us our... tram sessions.

MOTHER: He's only nine. He didn't know he was getting the words wrong.

FATHER *stands, menacing.*

AUNTIE PIE ACTOR: Everything that lived on earth held its breath.

ELIZA ACTOR: The sparrows on the windowsill choked on their trumpets.

JESUS ACTOR: The sun darkened and the sky shrank.

MOTHER: What are you doing?

FATHER: Out of the way, woman. I'm speaking to your son.

MOTHER *draws* THOMAS *protectively towards her.*

MOTHER: Please, Abel, he just made an honest mistake. I'll make sure he studies the hymns for next week. Abel…

FATHER *tries to drag* THOMAS *away from her.*

No! Please!

FATHER *slaps her savagely.* MOTHER *stifles a scream. The watching actors cover their eyes.*

AUNTIE PIE ACTOR: [*to the audience*] The angels in heaven covered their eyes, because that is what they do when a man hits his wife.

JESUS ACTOR: A deep sadness descended on the earth.

MARGOT: Pappa!

FATHER: Quiet! Thomas, go upstairs. And take the wooden spoon.

THOMAS *takes the wooden spoon and runs to his room. The watching actors slap their hands together, creating a rhythm.*

AUNTIE PIE ACTOR: The world was empty. Everything that had ever been had been taken away.

JESUS ACTOR: There was only noise.

ELIZA ACTOR: The sound of that slap on his mother's soft cheek.

AUNTIE PIE ACTOR: Thomas heard all the slaps his mother had ever received, a rain of slaps…

MOTHER ACTOR: … like the hail in Jan van Eyckstreet when the leaves were blasted from the trees.

THOMAS *presses his hands to his ears and speaks, fitting the words in between the slaps.*

THOMAS: God, please [*slap*] punish him [*slap*] with all the plagues [*slap*] of Egypt!

FATHER *enters the room.* THOMAS *stands.* FATHER *holds out his hand.* THOMAS *passes him the wooden spoon; he knows what is coming. He pulls down his trousers and bends over.* FATHER *beats* THOMAS *with the wooden spoon.* THOMAS *winces.*

AUNTIE PIE ACTOR: The pain cut like a knife through his skin.

ELIZA ACTOR: At first Thomas thought nothing, but then the words came flooding into his head.

THOMAS: HehitMamma! HehitMamma!

MARGOT ACTOR: Words and pain, the swish of the wooden spoon, more pain and more words…

MRS VAN AMERSFOORT ACTOR: Terrible words, that he had never thought before…

THOMAS: There-is-no-God. There-is-no-God!

> *The beating stops.*

FATHER: Lord God… repeat after me, Thomas!

THOMAS: Lord God…

FATHER: Have mercy on us miserable sinners.

THOMAS: Have mercy on us miserable sinners.

FATHER: And forgive us our transgressions!

THOMAS: And forgive us our transgressions.

FATHER: 'Lord have mercy on us miserable sinners and forgive us our transgressions.' You will stay here and repeat that one hundred times correctly, and then come downstairs.

> *He leaves the room.*

THOMAS: Dear God, will you please exist? All the plagues of Egypt, please, on Pappa. He hit Mamma, and it wasn't the first time! [*Calling*] God?!

AUNTIE PIE ACTOR: God was silent in every language.

JESUS ACTOR: The angels tried to dry their eyes.

ELIZA ACTOR: But their handkerchiefs were so full of tears that it began to rain, even in the desert.

SCENE FIVE

Music from a Dutch street organ or accordion, jaunty and loud. Children play in the street with a skipping rope.

THOMAS *writes in his book.*

THOMAS: *The Book of Everything.* On September 21st, 1951, Mrs van Amersfoort put a spell on the Bumbiter.

> MRS VAN AMERSFOORT *enters, carrying a heavy shopping bag. The children stop skipping to taunt her.*

CHILD: Hey, Mrs van Amersfoort, did you forget your broomstick?
CHILD: Where's your black cat, Mrs van Amersfoort?

> THOMAS *comes out into the street.*

CHILD: What's in the bag, Mrs van Amersfoort?
CHILD: Toad's guts for her witch's brew!
CHILD: Turn him into a frog, Mrs van Amersfoort! Go on, I dare you!

> *He grabs the bag, causing groceries to spill out at* THOMAS*'s feet.*

CHILD: Look out, she'll put a spell on you!

> *The* BUMBITER *enters, snarling and running around, trying to catch children, who scatter, shrieking.*

CHILDREN: The Bumbiter! The Bumbiter!

> *The* BUMBITER *corners* THOMAS. THOMAS *tries to run, but bumps into* MRS VAN AMERSFOORT. *The* BUMBITER *comes towards them, but* MRS VAN AMERSFOORT *stops him, raising her hands above her head, like an angry bear.*

MRS VAN AMERSFOORT: Stop! Stop!

> *The* BUMBITER *hesitates.*

> MRS VAN AMERSFOORT *mutters indistinct words at the growling* BUMBITER. *It sounds for all the world like a witch's incantation.*

That's enough of that, you silly bugger, settle down, settle down. Don't you snarl at me, boy, I'm up to your tricks. You won't get anywhere curling that lip; I've seen your teeth before. That'll do, I said, that'll do!

> *The* BUMBITER *backs off, whimpering.*

Yes, now go home! Home! You poor mad bugger, I know you can't help it. But go home, understand? Home!

> *The* BUMBITER *snarls. Then he wanders off.* THOMAS *is left with* MRS VAN AMERSFOORT. *He helps her to pick up the groceries.*

I've had it up to here with that nonsense. Thank you.

THOMAS: Can I carry your bag inside for you?

ELIZA ACTOR: He said it before he knew it.

> MRS VAN AMERSFOORT *stares at him, summing him up.*

AUNTIE PIE ACTOR: Thomas heard a hissing in his ears, then music he'd never heard before, with many violins. His heart pounded and he desperately hoped that Mrs van Amersfoort would say no.

THOMAS: Can I carry your bag inside for you?

MRS VAN AMERSFOORT: Thank you. That's very kind.

> THOMAS *has to make an enormous effort to lift the bag.*

It's not too heavy for you, is it? You're such a big boy.

> *A magic moment music chord. Suddenly* THOMAS *can lift the bag and he follows her along the street.*

SCENE SIX

THOMAS *follows* MRS VAN AMERSFOORT *and puts down the bag just inside the door.*

THOMAS: There you are.

> *He wants to go, but* MRS VAN AMERSFOORT *directs him further into the house.*

MRS VAN AMERSFOORT: Just put it over here.

> THOMAS *moves the bag and again turns to go, but she presses on.*

Sit anywhere you can, Thomas.

> *He sits, awkwardly.*

THOMAS: You know my name!

MRS VAN AMERSFOORT: We're neighbours, aren't we? Those walls are thin. I'm sorry about the mess. I'm a bit of a jackdaw, you see. I can't stop myself collecting paraphernalia—too much furniture, superfluous to my needs, bric-a-brac...

THOMAS: [*to the audience*] ... piles of newspapers and magazines and books; across the ceiling glided a huge bird with wings outstretched, and a black cat was sleeping on a globe of the world. Now I knew for certain that it was true. This was the house of a witch.

MRS VAN AMERSFOORT: It looks like a witch's house, doesn't it?

THOMAS: No. Not really. [*To the audience*] I didn't yet know if it was the scary house of a scary witch. That remained to be seen.

> MRS VAN AMERSFOORT *forces a glass of bright red liquid into* THOMAS*'s hand.*

MRS VAN AMERSFOORT: Here—you've earned a drink. Blood!

> THOMAS *hesitates—it looks like blood. She sees his distress and is amused.*

It's cordial, you silly goose!

> *She pours a slug from the bottle into a glass for herself, turning it red.*

THOMAS: Oh. Thank you, Missus.

> *They both drink.*

MRS VAN AMERSFOORT: It's damned nice to have you here. Damned nice. I don't get enough visitors. My children left home long ago, and I don't have a husband since… Oh no, you're too young to remember the War. The Nazis, they… executed my husband.

THOMAS: Oh. What's 'executed'?

MRS VAN AMERSFOORT: He was in the Resistance. Traitors gave him away—poor buggers were afraid for their own skins of course, so the Nazis caught him. They put him up against that wall out there, and they shot him dead.

THOMAS: Oh. I see.

AUNTIE PIE ACTOR: Thomas felt a terrible sadness in his throat and in his stomach. The same sadness he felt when, year in and year out, they nailed Jesus to the cross.

ELIZA ACTOR: He was always pleased when Jesus rose from his grave again, healthy and well.

MRS VAN AMERSFOORT: Mustn't dwell on it too much. Here, have you ever seen one of these?

> *She opens an old gramophone.*

THOMAS: A gramophone.

MRS VAN AMERSFOORT: Listen to this…

> *She puts on a record. A stream of beautiful, achingly sad violin music is heard, and continues as…* JESUS *appears, dressed as he is in the painting in* THOMAS*'s living room.*

JESUS: Hello, Thomas.

THOMAS: Hello… Lord Jesus.

JESUS: It's a cruel world, isn't it, Thomas? People executed, for nothing.

THOMAS: They… executed you too, Lord Jesus. They do it every Easter.

JESUS: [*smiling*] I won't let them nail me to that cross ever again. Damned if I will. I've had it up to here with that nonsense. Still, mustn't dwell on it too much. Only gets you down.

He disappears. The music continues.

MRS VAN AMERSFOORT: Beautiful, isn't it?

THOMAS: Yes.

MRS VAN AMERSFOORT: Beethoven. When I listen to this…

THOMAS: Me too.

AUNTIE PIE ACTOR: The globe of the world with the sleeping cat began to turn. Mrs van Amersfoort's heavy chair hung in the air above the floor, like a low cloud.

ELIZA ACTOR: Thomas dreamed he was soaring over green fields, and a castle with a Rolls Royce in the driveway. A fairytale princess, in a sky blue dress, a white collar and a leather leg, waved at him with her little finger. Her father stood on the battlements playing the violin, and her mother sang sweetly.

The music ends, but the record continues to scratch. MRS VAN AMERSFOORT *stares into the distance. A long uncomfortable pause.*

THOMAS: You've sure got a lot of books, Mrs van Amersfoort. What are they all about?

She snaps out of her trance and turns off the gramophone.

MRS VAN AMERSFOORT: Heavens! Books are about everything! Do you like reading?

THOMAS: Yes.

MRS VAN AMERSFOORT: Wait, maybe I've got something for you. [*She searches her bookshelves.*] What would you be interested in? What do you want to be when you grow up?

THOMAS: Happy. When I grow up I want to be happy.

A beat.

MRS VAN AMERSFOORT: That's a damned good idea. And where does happiness begin? With not being afraid anymore.

She hands him a book.

THOMAS: *Emil and the Detectives.*

MRS VAN AMERSFOORT: It's about a boy who doesn't want to be afraid, and who fights against injustice. You keep it.

THOMAS: Thank you.

MRS VAN AMERSFOORT: You were very brave today. You came inside with me, when all the other children say I'm a witch. They're right too. I am a witch.

The muffled voices of THOMAS'S FATHER *and* MOTHER *are heard off. We can't hear their exact words, but the impression is of an ugly domestic row.*

FATHER: [*off*] What do you mean, 'the money's never enough'?

MOTHER: [*off*] I do my best—you can't say I don't!

FATHER: [*off*] Any fool could do those books, you don't have to be Einstein!

MOTHER: [*off*] You could show enough respect not to call me a fool.

FATHER: [*off*] The way you behave, what else can I call you?

THOMAS *gets up.*

THOMAS: It's after five thirty. I have to go home. Thank you, Mrs van Amersfoort. [*He stops in the doorway.*] Thank you for everything.

MRS VAN AMERSFOORT: You're more than welcome, Thomas. You won't be afraid anymore?

THOMAS: Not of witches anyway.

He leaves.

Outside in the street THOMAS *comes face to face with* ELIZA.

ELIZA: Hello, Thomas.

THOMAS: Hello. Eliza.

He tries to leave.

ELIZA: What's wrong? Are you afraid?

THOMAS: Afraid?

ELIZA: Afraid to talk to me?

THOMAS: I… I have to go.

He runs off to escape into his house. She smiles and leaves.

SCENE SEVEN

MOTHER *and* FATHER *are at the dining table, poring over a ledger. The row has cooled but the atmosphere is tense.*

FATHER: How can twenty-five guilders just disappear?

MOTHER: I try to manage with the money you give me, but the prices in the shops go up all the time.

FATHER: It's so simple. Write down what you spend each day.

MOTHER: I do! But the shopkeepers don't always have time to write receipts and sometimes when I get home I forget how much I...

They look up as THOMAS *enters and try to compose themselves.*

I should get dinner ready.

FATHER: Finish the housekeeping budget first!

THOMAS *enters and goes to kiss* MOTHER. *She protects one cheek.*

THOMAS: The other cheek, Mamma.

MOTHER: Why?

THOMAS: Because.

He makes a point of kissing it particularly tenderly.

FATHER: Where did you get that book, Thomas?

THOMAS: [*mumbling*] From Mrs van Amersfoort.

FATHER: Who?

THOMAS: Mrs van Amersfoort.

FATHER: You just bumped into Mrs van Amersfoort and she said, 'Here's a book for you'?

THOMAS: It didn't happen like that.

FATHER: How did it happen then?

THOMAS: I carried her shopping bag inside.

MOTHER: How sweet of you! That poor woman is all alone...

FATHER: I don't want you going in there.

MOTHER: Why not?

FATHER: That woman is a communist. If the Russians come, she'll be cheering in the street. And we Christians will all be turned into slaves. What is the book?

THOMAS *puts it on the table.*

THOMAS: *Emil and the Detectives.*

FATHER *picks it up.*

FATHER: [*reading*] … by Erich Kastner. He's probably a communist too.
MOTHER: It's a children's book. What harm can it do?

FATHER *gives the book back to* THOMAS.

FATHER: You are to take it back tomorrow, Thomas. Then you are never
to go there again, understand?
MOTHER: Can I make the supper now?
FATHER: So how are we going to meet the housekeeping budget this
month?
MOTHER: I'll make it up out of my clothing allowance.
FATHER: No need for that. Here.

He gives her a banknote.

Next time, make that housekeeping money last.
MOTHER: I will.

THOMAS *goes to his room.*

THOMAS: The best place for thinking is beside an open window. [*He
writes.*] *The Book of Everything…* Dear Eliza, maybe you think
you're not pretty because you've got a leather leg that creaks when
you walk. But you are the prettiest girl in the world. I think one
day you will live in a castle with a Rolls Royce in the driveway.
I'm not writing this because I want to be your boyfriend. I know
that's impossible because you are sixteen, and I am only nine…
[*crossing this out and replacing it with…*] nearly ten. I am writing
this because it is true. [*Looking up*] I'll never be brave enough to
really write that to Eliza.

MOTHER *approaches.*

MOTHER: Thomas.

THOMAS *quickly hides his book and pretends to be reading* Emil
and the Detectives.

THOMAS: Mamma.

She picks up the novel and flips the pages.

MOTHER: Mrs van Amersfoort's husband gave his life for our freedom,
and she saved people from the Nazis too. When they shot Mr van
Amersfoort, the Nazis made us all watch, to teach us a lesson.

THOMAS: Was I there? And Margot?

MOTHER: Yes, you were just a baby in my arms. As far as I'm concerned, you can go in there any time.

THOMAS: [*surprised*] Good.

But Pappa said—

MOTHER: Don't let your father find out.

A beat.

THOMAS: Mamma, are you happy?

MOTHER: Yes, Thomas. I'm happy because you make me happy. You're my little hero.

She ruffles his hair and leaves. THOMAS *writes again, on a loose sheet of paper this time.*

THOMAS: Dear Eliza, I don't dare to write this, but I'm doing it anyway. Maybe you think you're not pretty because you've got a leather leg...

The watching actors speak snippets from the letter to Eliza, overlapping the words, ending with '... I am writing this because it is true.'

The violin music is repeated as THOMAS *completes his letter, folds it, and adds on the back...*

For Eliza.

SCENE EIGHT

THOMAS *takes the letter into the street and arrives at a postbox. He's about to drop the letter into it, then hesitates.*

MRS VAN AMERSFOORT *appears.*

MRS VAN AMERSFOORT: Where does happiness begin? With not being afraid anymore.

THOMAS: That's easy for you to say. You're a witch.

MRS VAN AMERSFOORT: Maybe I became a witch because I'm not afraid anymore.

THOMAS *jams the letter into the postbox. It is immediately carried away, passing through several sets of hands, then flying through the sky, arriving in the hands of* ELIZA. THOMAS *runs back inside and reads* Emil and the Detectives.

AUNTIE PIE ACTOR: Thomas wouldn't be able to go outside now, not ever again. What would he do if he met Eliza in the street? Maybe he could try ducking into a doorway, or hiding behind a fat lady, like Emil did in *Emil and the Detectives*.

THOMAS: [*to the audience*] *Emil and the Detectives* isn't a book about God. It's about a German boy in Berlin. It seems that Emil never has to go to church, which is weird. He's worried about crooks stealing his money. [*He reads.*] 'Emil took a pin that he found in his lapel, stuck it through the envelope and banknotes and finally through the lining of his jacket. You might say that he had nailed the money tight. "There," he thought, "now nothing can happen".'

> MARGOT *enters.*

MARGOT: Thomas, what was it like there?

THOMAS: Where?

MARGOT: At the witch's house.

THOMAS: How would I know?

MARGOT: I know very well you went inside.

> *She grabs the scruff of his neck, then 'tortures' him.* THOMAS *is in pain but resists valiantly.*

I'll *make* you tell me, you pathetic little invertebrate!

THOMAS: No you won't, you… superfluous bric-a-brac!

> MARGOT *is amused. She releases him.*

MARGOT: Go on. What was it like?

THOMAS: Different.

MARGOT: What do you mean 'different'?

THOMAS: Different from here.

MOTHER: [*off*] Thomas, Margot, dinner's ready!

MARGOT: We'll talk… soon.

> *She propels him towards the dining room, where they join* MOTHER *and* FATHER *at the table.* FATHER *sharpens a carving knife on a steel.*

That's a razor sharp knife, eh, Pap?

FATHER: You could skin an old cow with this.

MARGOT: [*making slicing actions with relish*] Slit, slash, straight through.

FATHER: If there's one thing I hate, it's a blunt knife. [*He finishes sharpening.*] Let us pray. Lord God… we thank Thee for Thy bountiful gifts. Thou givest us each day our daily bread, and You minister also to our spiritual wants, forgiving all our sins, including those we name now in the silence of our hearts…

As he continues to mutter the prayer, JESUS *appears.*

JESUS: Hey, Thomas. How's it going?

THOMAS: Good, Lord Jesus.

JESUS: Just good or extra good?

THOMAS: Just good.

JESUS: Don't be afraid, little feller. You can tell me. And I won't pass it on. Cross my heart and hope to die.

THOMAS *takes in the implications of this.*

THOMAS: He shouldn't hit Mamma.

JESUS: Who shouldn't hit Mamma?

THOMAS: You know.

JESUS: I know nothing and my lips are sealed.

THOMAS: That's what Grandpa always says!

JESUS *smiles and shrugs.*

I'm talking about Pappa hitting Mamma.

JESUS: God Almighty! Has he got a screw loose or what?

THOMAS: That's what Auntie Pie always says!

FATHER: In the name of our Lord Jesus Christ.

JESUS: That'll be me. Gotta go.

MOTHER & MARGOT: [*together*] Amen.

He disappears.

MOTHER: Smakelijk eten allemaal [*pronounced 'Smarklick ayter, ullermarl'*].

ALL: Smakelijk eten.

THOMAS: [*to the audience*] That's Dutch for 'tuck in'.

The doorbell rings.

MOTHER: Could somebody answer that please?

THOMAS *goes to the door and returns with a letter.*

THOMAS: Eliza has written back to me already! If it's an angry letter, I don't want to go on living. I'll drown myself in the canal with the tropical guppies. [*He examines the letter.*] 'To Mr A. Klopper'— that's not me, that's my father. 'From Mrs van Amersfoort.' This is even worse! A national disaster! Mrs van Amersfoort is a witch and an economist too. Who'll get the blame if Pappa reads this? Thomas! Or Mamma.

MOTHER: Thomas, your dinner's getting cold.

FATHER: Thomas!

THOMAS: I'll have to tear it up. [*He tears the envelope and a letter falls out. He picks it up and reads it.*] 'A man who hits his wife dishonours himself.'

MOTHER: Thomas, what are you doing?

THOMAS: Just a minute!

> *He stuffs the letter in his pocket.*

AUNTIE PIE ACTOR: Why were his fingers shaking?

JESUS ACTOR: Why did his stomach feel as if he'd swallowed a hippopotamus?

AUNTIE PIE: Because he was doing something that was absolutely forbidden.

> THOMAS *returns to the table.*

MOTHER: Who was there, Thomas?

THOMAS: Just… some little kids. Mucking about.

> MOTHER *knows something is going on.* FATHER *opens the Bible.*

FATHER: Let us hear the word of the Lord. [*He reads.*] 'And the Lord said unto Moses: Pharaoh's heart is hardened, he will not let the people go. Behold I will strike with my rod the water of the Nile, and it shall be turned into blood. And all the fishes that are in the river shall die.'

THOMAS: The guppies too? It wasn't the fishes' fault that the pharaoh was a bad man.

FATHER: What did you say, Thomas?

THOMAS: The pharaoh was a bad man.

FATHER: Yes, and God turned the water to blood to warn the pharaoh against doing wrong. That was the first plague of Egypt. Tomorrow we'll read about the second. In the name of our Lord Jesus Christ. Amen.

All clear the table and leave. THOMAS *is alone.*

THOMAS: God turned the water to blood?

SCENE NINE

More street activities and bright music.

AUNTIE PIE ACTOR: The letter from Mrs van Amersfoort was burning a hole in Thomas's pocket.

THOMAS: 'A man who hits his wife dishonours himself.' Maybe it's a magic spell. A spell that can change people into something different. If I could keep this... somewhere secret... [*noticing the book*] like Emil did!

> *He fumbles in his pocket, finds a safety pin, and pins the letter inside his shirt.* ELIZA *appears.*

ELIZA: [*calling*] Thomas!

THOMAS: Oh no!

> THOMAS *tries to escape.*

> ELIZA *tries to whistle through her fingers to capture his attention. She fails at the first attempt and the watching* JESUS ACTOR *does it for her.* THOMAS *stops.*

Oh, hi.

ELIZA: I got your letter.

> *She holds it up.*

THOMAS: Oh.

ELIZA: Listen, Thomas... This is the most... the most beautiful letter anyone ever sent me.

THOMAS: Oh.

ELIZA: I'm going to keep it forever. And I'll read it whenever I'm sad.

THOMAS: Oh.

ELIZA: You're a really sweet boy. When I'm living in my castle, you come and visit any time. I'll take you for a ride in my Rolls Royce.

> *She kisses him on the cheek.*

AUNTIE PIE: It was amazing! A kiss from Eliza in the middle of the street. For a letter! Thomas jumped for joy and to his amazement he was so light he rose two metres into the air.

THOMAS: I must write letters to everybody. It makes them happy. And it makes them like me.

> THOMAS *runs, jumps, runs, then stops and enters Mrs van Amersfoort's house.*

> MRS VAN AMERSFOORT *pours* THOMAS *a glass of red cordial.*

I finished reading *Emil and the Detectives.*

MRS VAN AMERSFOORT: And?

THOMAS: I liked how the children all helped Emil, and how they caught the crook. That idea of pinning the letter inside his shirt was really good too.

MRS VAN AMERSFOORT: The letter?

THOMAS: I mean the money. [*Pause.*] Can I ask you something? It's a bit of a weird question really.

MRS VAN AMERSFOORT: I have a weird question for you too. Your one first.

THOMAS: Can I take the cordial home with me?

MRS VAN AMERSFOORT: Why not just drink it here?

THOMAS: I mean the whole bottle.

MRS VAN AMERSFOORT: Why do you want the whole bottle?

> *Then seeing that* THOMAS *is hesitant about answering…*

Fine, I'll buy another one.

THOMAS: Thank you.

MRS VAN AMERSFOORT: Now my weird question. Here it comes. Thomas, do you get hit at home?

AUNTIE PIE ACTOR: The shock was like a kick in the stomach.

ELIZA ACTOR: The cat jumped off the globe of the world and stretched.

MRS VAN AMERSFOORT: Do you get hit, Thomas?

THOMAS: Me? No.

> *Long pause.*

> *The actors and* MRS VAN AMERSFOORT *watch* THOMAS *attentively.*

[*To the audience*] I just get a spanking sometimes. It's Mamma who gets hit. Jesus, Mamma what should I do? [*He shakes his head. To* MRS VAN AMERSFOORT] No. Not me.

MRS VAN AMERSFOORT: That's good. Shall we listen to some more music?

THOMAS: I have to go soon.

MRS VAN AMERSFOORT: Fine. Let's see if there's another book for you. [*She takes one from the shelf.*] Aha! This one I want back. It's called *Alone in the World*, but I'm lending it to you to show you that you're not alone in the world.

THOMAS: Thanks. Can I take the cordial?

He takes the bottle and leaves, then enters his own house and sneaks to the fish tank.

All the plagues of Egypt, God! Please, please, please God, I humbly beseech thee, if you do exist, smite Pappa with all the plagues of Egypt!

He pours the cordial into the fish tank, turning the water bright red. He then hides the bottle. MARGOT *enters, and screams.*

MARGOT: The water's been turned to blood!

FATHER, MOTHER *and* THOMAS *run on and look at the fish tank in horror.*

Blackout.

END OF ACT ONE

ACT TWO

SCENE TEN

Music.

MARGOT *enters and screams.*
Suddenly we're back to a reprise of the action at the end of Act One.

MARGOT: The water's been turned to blood!

MOTHER: What happened?

MARGOT: Oh no, it's a plague of Egypt right here in Amsterdam South.

THOMAS: Goodness! That's impossible!

MOTHER: You'll have to change that water, Thomas.

FATHER: No, that water stays right there.

MARGOT: [*stifling giggles*] It's a miraculous Act of God!

FATHER: In the time of the pharaoh there were tricksters who turned the
    Nile water red. The pharaoh's magicians. They said, 'If God can do
    it, so can we'.

MARGOT: How did they do that then?

FATHER: I don't know, but they were sent by the devil, that is certain.

MOTHER: Maybe there's some sort of bacteria in the water.

FATHER: I don't think so. I think the bacterium is in this room. A human
    bacterium, who thinks it is funny to mock God's almighty power.

MARGOT: A magician!

FATHER: An imposter, like the pharaoh's magicians.

MARGOT: Hey, this is exciting, Pappa.

MOTHER: I'll change the water after dinner.

FATHER: You'll do no such thing. 'The fish died and began to stink':
    that's what it says in the Good Book.

    There is a tense pause.

MARGOT: We read a good book at school last week. It's about this boy
    who finds a magic sword that gives him special powers...

FATHER: This is not a joke, Margot. There is only one true book in this
    world and that is the Bible. The books you read at school are written
    by sinful people who are like the pharaoh's magicians. They write
    books, but they are false books.

MARGOT: Oh.

FATHER: Read them wisely and take care that your heart belongs to the Bible. [*He opens the Bible and reads.*] 'Then God said to Moses, "Go to the pharaoh and tell him to let my people go. And if he will not, then I will send a plague of frogs. The Nile shall swarm with frogs, and they shall force their way into his house, and into his bed, everywhere the frogs shall come." And so it came to pass, that the frogs covered the land of Egypt. But the magicians did the same with their rods, and they too summoned the frogs, through the whole land of Egypt.'

He marks the spot and closes the Bible. MOTHER *rises.*

MARGOT: They were clever, those magicians.

FATHER: The devil is terribly clever.

> MOTHER *fetches a bucket and a rubber hose.*

What are you doing?

MOTHER: Changing the water.

FATHER: What did I say?

MOTHER: If we don't change it, the guppies will die.

FATHER: A good lesson for our evil sorcerer.

MOTHER: I don't think so.

FATHER: You heard what I said, woman. Stop that immediately!

MARGOT: Pappa, can you help me with my geometry?

FATHER: I'm counting to three. One, two… three!

MARGOT: Pappa!

> FATHER *steps up to* MOTHER *and slaps her. She recoils, then deliberately hits back, furiously swinging at him, seldom connecting. But he is stronger and knocks her to the ground.*

MARGOT: [*yelling*] Pappa, the Bible was written by people! Not by God, by people!

The doorbell rings. Silence.

FATHER: Who could that be?

THOMAS: Lord Jesus.

> FATHER *kneels by* MOTHER.

FATHER: Upstairs. Here, take a handkerchief.

MOTHER *leaves. The bell rings again and* MRS VAN AMERSFOORT *is heard offstage.*

MRS VAN AMERSFOORT: [*off*] Neighbour? Could I borrow a cup of sugar?

FATHER: Certainly, Mrs van Amersfoort. I'll bring it out to you.

He hurries to get a cup of sugar. But MARGOT *goes to open the door and* MRS VAN AMERSFOORT *enters, a cup in her hand.* FATHER *returns with the sugar.*

Oh, you brought a cup.

He pours sugar into her cup.

MRS VAN AMERSFOORT: Is your wife not here?

FATHER: She's not feeling well.

MRS VAN AMERSFOORT: Oh dear, what's the problem?

FATHER: Stomach ache.

THOMAS: [*to the audience*] It was amazing. Pappa was afraid!

MRS VAN AMERSFOORT: Maybe we should have a talk.

FATHER: A talk?

MRS VAN AMERSFOORT: Think about it. Hey, Thomas. Give your mother a kiss from me. Thank you for the sugar.

She leaves. FATHER *sinks to his knees and prays.*

FATHER: Lord God, forgive me for losing my control. What must I do to bring this family to you? Help your humble servant, O Lord, this I pray, in the name of our Lord Jesus Christ. Amen.

THOMAS: I'm going upstairs. Shall I take the wooden spoon?

FATHER: No, son. Come here.

He reaches out his arm, but THOMAS *steps back and goes to where* MOTHER *lies, her back to him.* FATHER *and* MARGOT *leave.*

MOTHER: Please don't do that again, Thomas. No more plagues of Egypt, all right?

THOMAS: No, Mamma. [*He goes to sit by the window and prays.*] Lord God, don't forgive him. Never forgive him!

JESUS *appears.*

JESUS: Hey, Thomas, everything tickety-boo?

THOMAS: No.

JESUS: Why? What's up?

THOMAS: To tell the truth, we don't like you very much just now, Lord Jesus.

JESUS: Hey, what's all this? Didn't I save humanity?

THOMAS: Save us from what, may I ask?

JESUS: Well, you know...

THOMAS: I know nothing and my lips are sealed.

> JESUS *laughs.*

JESUS: Okay, okay, you'll understand when you grow up.

THOMAS: If you say so, Lord Jesus.

JESUS: I'm glad you exist, Thomas. You're strong, Thomas, strong because you're kind. Will you remember that? We up there are very proud of you. Do you believe me?

THOMAS: Yes, Lord Jesus.

JESUS: Hey, just call me 'Jesus'. Whatcha reading? [*He picks up the book.*] *Alone in the World.* They can't mean you, Thomas. You're my favourite boy. You're not alone in the world. And my angels can't wait to meet you in heaven.

> *This doesn't sound too good to* THOMAS, *but he politely answers.*

THOMAS: Oh. Great!

> JESUS *would like to stay, but has run out of things to say. It's getting a bit awkward as he backs off.*

JESUS: Yes, well...

THOMAS: Nice of you to drop in... Jesus.

> JESUS *smiles shyly, waves and disappears.*

SCENE ELEVEN

THOMAS *writes in his book.*

THOMAS: I remember everything. I forget nothing. I write everything down so that later I'll know exactly what happened. One day in 1951, the frogs came.

> *The sound of many frogs croaking. In the original production dozens of green table tennis balls were bounced on to the stage here.*

At first I thought the street had turned green. But then I saw it was moving. The Breughelstreet was covered with frogs. So was the Apollo Lane.

AUNTIE PIE ACTOR: The frogs gathered by the door.

ELIZA ACTOR: They climbed on each others' backs and piled themselves high against the wall of the house. The smell of canal water was overpowering.

AUNTIE PIE ACTOR: Thousands of frogs, drumming on the front door like a million fingers.

THOMAS: [*calling*] I didn't do it, Mamma! I had nothing to do with it! [*He calls out the window.*] Hello, frogs! Hello, I'm Thomas! Mamma doesn't want any more plagues of Egypt! So go back to the creeks and canals. Please!

The frog sound dies down. In the original production ACTORS *swept up the table tennis balls with brooms.*

JESUS ACTOR: Jesus swept.

ELIZA ACTOR: It was quiet, way into the far distance. The front door stopped shaking.

MARGOT *enters and sees* THOMAS *talking out the window.*

THOMAS: Thank you, frogs. Thank you for coming.

MARGOT: Thomas, what are you doing?

THOMAS: Shhh!

MARGOT: What were you doing?

THOMAS: There were frogs—heaps of them. But Mamma doesn't want the plagues of Egypt.

MARGOT: Thomas, how many frogs were there?

THOMAS: Millions.

MARGOT: Really? Did you see them yourself?

THOMAS: With my own eyes.

MARGOT *puts an arm around his shoulders.*

MARGOT: You can't always believe your eyes. Thomas, you mustn't let things get to you.

THOMAS: No.

MARGOT: Thomas?

THOMAS: Yes?

MARGOT: You know what Eliza said to me? 'You've got a really nice brother.'

THOMAS: Oh.

MARGOT: And you know what? Eliza's right.

She sits next to him.

THOMAS: What does 'dishonour' mean?

MARGOT: It means losing your honour. For example... I can't think of an example.

THOMAS: Doesn't matter. But what's honour?

MARGOT: Wait, I know. It means losing your dignity.

THOMAS: Ah. What's dignity? [*He pulls out the letter and reads.*] 'A man who hits his wife dishonours himself.'

MARGOT *takes the letter.*

MARGOT: Who gave you this? This is sooo true!

THOMAS: Not telling. It's a secret.

MARGOT: Pappa has to read this!

THOMAS: What if he gets angry?

MARGOT: He must. He really has to.

THOMAS: Not yet.

MARGOT *watches as he pins the letter inside his shirt again.*

SCENE TWELVE

FATHER *enters, back home from work. He goes through his routine of hanging up his coat.*

FATHER: I'm home!

MOTHER, THOMAS *and* MARGOT *enter.* MOTHER *has a wad of cotton in her nose.* FATHER *takes something from his coat pocket.*

Look what I found on the doorstep. A frog!

He examines it and shows it to them.

The poor little creature is so scared he's got his hands in front of his eyes. Here, off you go, little feller!

Quite gently he releases the frog out the door.

MARGOT: Something funny happened to me today too. I was sent out of my Dutch Literature class.

FATHER: Hey? Why was that?

MARGOT: Mr de Rijp said I was a know-all, and he chucked me out.

THOMAS: What's a know-all?

FATHER: Someone who thinks he knows better about everything, and that is very annoying. What exactly did you say to Mr de Rijp?

MARGOT: I told Mr de Rijp I wasn't reading the sinful books on our library list. I said the Bible was enough for me; other books are false.

FATHER: Now, um, listen to me, Margot. You misunderstood me. In the books you have to read at school, there are opinions of men. In the Bible, you don't find opinions, but truths. Because the Bible is God's word.

MARGOT: That's exactly what I told Mr de Rijp.

FATHER: That doesn't mean that you have to give cheek to your teacher. Tomorrow—

MARGOT: I was only saying what you taught me.

FATHER: Tomorrow—

MARGOT: What's for dinner, Mam?

MOTHER: Pea soup.

FATHER: Tomorrow, you will go to Mr de Rijp and apologise.

MARGOT: Sure. Do you want me to do your hair tonight, Mam?

MOTHER: Lovely.

FATHER: What is this world coming to? You will read all the books that you should read, understand?

MARGOT: Yes, Pap. I could braid it for you, Mam.

MOTHER: That would be good, Margot.

THOMAS *pulls out his book.*

THOMAS: Do you know *Alone in the World*? It's about a boy who's alone in the world. It's sad, but exciting too.

MOTHER: Help me in the kitchen, Thomas.

FATHER: [*to* MOTHER] Why don't you say something? She's your daughter too.

MOTHER: Oh, you say it so much better than I can.

FATHER: [*to* THOMAS] Where did you get that book?

MARGOT: From me.

FATHER: Oh. And who gave it to you?

MARGOT: Santa Claus. Years ago.

FATHER: Let us pray. Lord God, we beg Thy forgiveness for our innumerable sins. Please lead us in Thy ways, and teach us to follow Thy paths, that we may truly be Thy servants. You see our weaknesses and You know that we too often are tempted to forsake righteousness...

As he continues his muttered prayer, JESUS *appears.*

JESUS: Listen, Thomas...

THOMAS: Oh hi, Jesus.

JESUS: ... I had problems with my father too. Ooh, he was a strict old codger! I had to get nailed on that cross whether I liked it or not.

THOMAS: I suppose that wasn't nice.

JESUS: No, it was not. Once and never again. And now I've lost Him.

THOMAS: Who?

JESUS: God the Father. I can't find him anywhere. He's not in heaven— weird. He disappeared after you got your last beating. It was too much for him.

THOMAS: Do you think so?

JESUS: I think he loved you, Thomas, and he couldn't stand watching that anymore. That's my personal opinion.

FATHER: Hear the Word of the Lord...

JESUS: I've heard this one.

He turns to leave.

THOMAS: See you, Jesus.

FATHER *opens the Bible to read.*

FATHER: 'Behold, I will send swarms of flies upon thee, and upon thy servants, and upon thy people, and into thy houses: and the houses of the Egyptians shall be full of swarms of flies, and also the ground whereon they are.'

The doorbell rings. THOMAS *goes to answer it.*

SCENE THIRTEEN

AUNTIE PIE *enters.*

AUNTIE PIE: Hello, my dear boy!

THOMAS: Hello, Auntie Pie.

She hugs him.

AUNTIE PIE: Oh, aren't you a sweet little sausage! Everything tickety-boo?

She releases THOMAS, *then as* FATHER, MOTHER *and* MARGOT
approach, she announces...

Benno hit me! And you know why? Because I bought a pair of slacks.
My husband hit me for wearing trousers! Has he got a screw loose or
what?

FATHER: Margot and Thomas, go to your rooms. Auntie Pie and I have
something to discuss.

AUNTIE PIE: Oh no, everyone ought to know about this. Margot, Thomas,
your Uncle Ben hit your Auntie Pie for wearing trousers. There!

MOTHER: Sit down, Pie. Would you like some coffee?

    AUNTIE PIE *sits.*

AUNTIE PIE: And now I think that you, [*pointing to* FATHER] as his
oldest brother, should talk to him and tell him this is not right.
Otherwise I'm standing outside our house with a placard—'Mr
Klopper hits his wife for wearing trousers'. I mean, has he got a
screw loose or what?

FATHER: Calm down, Pie. It is in fact the case that the man is the head
of the family...

AUNTIE PIE: That doesn't mean that he has to go round slapping people
willy-nilly.

FATHER: Hear me out, Pie. It's the man's duty to lead and guide his wife
and children. If they won't listen to him, what else can he do but...?

AUNTIE PIE: Belt them?

FATHER: ... be firm with them! That is what God has ordained. God has
also ordained that women wear skirts and men wear trousers...

    This sounds like total nonsense to AUNTIE PIE.

AUNTIE PIE: What are you talking about?

FATHER: ... and if you so stubbornly resist God's will, your husband
has the right, indeed the duty, to use a firm hand to bring you to
righteousness.

AUNTIE PIE: Really? I see you're completely useless. But I'm telling
you, if he hits me one more time I'm leaving and never coming back.
And from now on I'm only wearing trousers! You watch me. [*With a
wink to* THOMAS] What do you reckon, sausage? [*To* MOTHER] What
happened to your nose? I hope you didn't resist God's will?

MOTHER: No.

AUNTIE PIE: Only joking. How did you get that fat nose then?

MOTHER: I just... bumped into something.

MARGOT: The fish tank, eh Pap?

THOMAS: [*aside*] Don't do it, Margot. Don't give cheek!

AUNTIE PIE: [*measured*] Yes, they can be dangerous, those fish tanks. I'm personally always bumping into them, especially with my nose.

MOTHER: Shall I put the kettle on?

AUNTIE PIE: Not for me. I've just seen the light. [*To* FATHER] You're as much of a coward as your brother.

MOTHER: Pie, you've got it wrong.

AUNTIE PIE: Duty calls. Back to my pious husband with his flapping hands. But I'll teach him. I'll fix him myself!

She kisses MOTHER, MARGOT *and finally* THOMAS.

We won't let them walk over us, will we, sausage?

She leaves.

FATHER: Don't you have homework to do, Margot?

MARGOT: Yes I do, Pap. But first I'm doing Mamma's hair.

He wants to enforce his will, but can't.

FATHER: I have to finish some work for the office.

He leaves.

SCENE FOURTEEN

In Mrs van Amersfoort's house, THOMAS *returns the book* Alone in the World.

THOMAS: Thank you for lending me the book, Mrs van Amersfoort.

MRS VAN AMERSFOORT: You've finished it already?

THOMAS: I read it twice.

MRS VAN AMERSFOORT: I'm impressed. You must be a damn good reader. Oh, how did you like the frogs?

THOMAS: [*smiling*] Good. But Mamma doesn't like them.

MRS VAN AMERSFOORT: I can imagine. I just did it for fun. It's actually a pretty bloody clumsy plague, that frog one. Hey, listen to this. This is good. You've got a fish tank, haven't you?

She takes a new book and reads from 'The Guppy' by Ogden Nash.

How do you like it?

THOMAS: Funny.

MRS VAN AMERSFOORT: I love Ogden Nash. He's very amusing, for an American.

THOMAS: Oh. But what does it mean?

MRS VAN AMERSFOORT: Nothing. It's just fun.

THOMAS: [*doubtful*] Oh, I see.

MRS VAN AMERSFOORT: Music doesn't have to mean anything. It's just beautiful. The forest and the beach don't mean anything. Forest is forest and beach is beach. You can just enjoy them, can't you?

THOMAS: Yes. We sometimes go to Zandvoort Beach for the day.

MRS VAN AMERSFOORT: And how is that?

THOMAS: Great.

MRS VAN AMERSFOORT: And what does Zandvoort Beach mean?

THOMAS: Nothing. It's just great.

MRS VAN AMERSFOORT: Would you read to me? Now? Here?

She gives him the book.

THOMAS: But this is a kids' book.

MRS VAN AMERSFOORT: Begin at the beginning.

THOMAS *reads, hesitatingly at first, then with more confidence, from 'The Sniffle' by Ogden Nash.*

As he reads, MRS VAN AMERSFOORT *really gets into it, laughing loudly and at times quoting along with him.*

ELIZA ACTOR: Mrs van Amersfoort was a witch, but now she was under a spell herself. As Thomas read on, he saw that she wasn't an old lady, but a young girl, her hair in plaits with bows on them. Any minute she could jump up and grab a skipping rope.

THOMAS *finishes reading.*

MRS VAN AMERSFOORT: That was marvellous, Thomas! My husband always used to read aloud to me. I loved that.

THOMAS: Maybe we could start a Reading Out Loud Club.

MRS VAN AMERSFOORT: Good idea.

THOMAS: With music in the intervals.

MRS VAN AMERSFOORT: We'd need a program.

THOMAS: And I could recite Psalm 22. I know that off by heart. 'My

God, my God, why hast thou forsaken me? Why art thou so far from helping me, and from the words of my roaring? O my God, I cry in the day time, but thou hearest not; and in the night season, and am not silent.'

MRS VAN AMERSFOORT: Whacko the diddly-oh! That's brilliant. And so nice for children, don't you think?

THOMAS: It's hard to learn it all out of your head.

MRS VAN AMERSFOORT: I could never do it. But right, we've got a Reading Out Loud Club and a program. We'll do it here. You read from Ogden Nash and I'll organise the audience.

THOMAS: Great.

MRS VAN AMERSFOORT: Take the book home, then you can practise.

THOMAS: Whacko the diddly-oh!

He leaves.

SCENE FIFTEEN

THOMAS *sits and writes.*

THOMAS: *The Book of Everything.* The next day seemed like an ordinary day, but that was because I wasn't paying attention. Good things happened on that day too. Like when I met Eliza in the street.

ELIZA: Hello, Thomas.

THOMAS: Hello, Eliza.

He springs up and tries to escape again, as shyness overcomes him, but this time...

ELIZA: Come here, my darling friend.

She hugs him.

THOMAS: Girls are really nice. Maybe Eliza won't be able to get a boyfriend because she's got a leather leg. Maybe she'll wait for me till I'm bigger.

ELIZA *releases him.*

ELIZA: I heard from Mrs van Amersfoort that you can read aloud really well. I'd love to see that.

She leaves.

THOMAS: I'll wait for you, forever. [*He runs back inside.*] Hey, Mam.

MOTHER: Hey, my little dreamer. I saw Mrs van Amersfoort this morning.

THOMAS *feels for the letter under his shirt.*

THOMAS: Oh.

MOTHER: She says you're starting a Reading Out Loud Club. That's nice.

THOMAS: Yes, I have to practise.

MOTHER: You don't want a glass of milk?

THOMAS: No.

MOTHER: You're becoming such a big grown-up boy these days, aren't you?

THOMAS: Sort of.

MOTHER: My little hero!

THOMAS *goes to his room, unpins the letter from his shirt and reads.*

THOMAS: 'A man who hits his wife dishonours himself.' I don't like cowards, but I am one all the same. I'm not brave enough to do what has to be done.

JESUS *appears.*

JESUS: You are, you know.

THOMAS: Oh Lord Jesus, let this buck pass from me. You said that when you had to die. Don't let me be a chicken.

JESUS: Follow me.

JESUS *directs him towards the table.* THOMAS *sneaks to the table.* MARGOT *enters and watches.*

AUNTIE PIE ACTOR: The world held its breath.

ELIZA ACTOR: Would Thomas dare to do it?

AUNTIE PIE ACTOR: The world didn't know.

THOMAS *lays the letter in the Bible, shuts it and leaves it on the table.* MARGOT *gives* THOMAS *the 'thumbs up' sign. So does* JESUS, *before leaving.* MARGOT *and* THOMAS *sit at the table.*

The sound of, or music like, a ticking time bomb. FATHER *enters.*

FATHER: I'm home!

He goes through his coat hanging routine, then comes to the table.

MOTHER *enters with (mimed) soup bowls, and they all sit, eating the 'soup'. There is a strong ritualised feeling to what they are doing. The bomb ticks on.*

When they finish, FATHER *opens the Bible, spots the letter and picks it up.*

What's this? [*He reads the letter.*] So. Good, I'll read you what it says. 'A man who hits his wife dishonours himself.' I agree completely, but there's one thing missing. A man who hits his wife without reason dishonours himself.

MARGOT *hums 'Zippity Doo Dah'.*

Could you turn off that music for a moment, Margot?

MARGOT: Yeah, Pap. Sorry.

FATHER: That letter itself is not important. It seems that someone wants to turn us against each other. Someone wants to turn us away from God and His commandments. The question is, who put it inside the Bible? [*Pause.*] Nobody?

AUNTIE PIE ACTOR: It was as if all life on earth had died, it was so quiet. So quiet the dead awoke in the churchyard. They pricked up their ears, but they heard nothing.

FATHER: Someone at this table is a traitor. I don't know who it is, but nothing is hidden from God. Let us ask for His help. [*He prays.*] Almighty God, help this family to be strong in these times of temptation...

THOMAS: Jesus?

JESUS *appears.*

JESUS: I'm here.

THOMAS *opens his eyes.*

He means well, I think. But he's scared. He's actually a chicken, if you ask me.

THOMAS: I don't know.

JESUS: He's hiding like a scared child behind God's broad back.

FATHER: This we pray in the name of our Lord Jesus Christ. Amen.

JESUS: I'm with you.

JESUS *waves and leaves.* THOMAS *waves back.*

FATHER: What are you doing, Thomas?

THOMAS: Waving to Jesus.

FATHER slams his hand on the Bible.

FATHER: I won't put up with this! In my house, no-one makes jokes about our Lord and Saviour!

THOMAS: It wasn't a joke.

FATHER: Do you understand?

THOMAS: Yes, Pappa.

FATHER: And now I want to know who put this letter in the Bible.

MARGOT: I did.

She hums another line of 'Zippity Doo Dah'.

FATHER: I don't believe a word of it.

MARGOT shrugs.

Who wrote it then? I don't recognise the handwriting.

MARGOT: Found it in the street.

She hums again.

FATHER: You're lying. We know very well who put it there.

He looks at MOTHER.

MOTHER: Yes. I did it.

Pause, then THOMAS springs to his feet.

THOMAS: That's not true! I did it!

FATHER: You are a liar, Thomas.

THOMAS: I did it! I did it! There are holes in the letter—I made them with this safety pin. There!

He throws the pin on the table.

FATHER: It's true. There are holes. You didn't lie, Thomas. I accused you unjustly. Forgive me. But what is more important is that someone has used you. Someone is trying to turn you against your father. Who wrote this letter? Auntie Pie?

THOMAS: That's a secret.

FATHER: Thomas, take the wooden spoon and wait for me upstairs.

MOTHER: That's not going to happen. Thomas will stay here and you can read from the Bible.

AUNTIE PIE ACTOR: A hot wind screamed across the earth. The trees withered and the animals fled.

ELIZA ACTOR: Everything was destroyed and empty. Nothing could live on the earth.

FATHER: Thomas, get the wooden spoon.

MOTHER: No!

MARGOT *hums again.*

THOMAS: I'll get the spoon, Mamma.

MOTHER: My brave little hero is staying here.

She puts her arms around THOMAS.

FATHER: Don't you contradict me, woman!

THOMAS: Let me go, Mamma.

MOTHER: You don't deserve any punishment.

MARGOT *hums to the tune of 'Zippity Do Dah' again.*

FATHER: Let that child go.

MOTHER: No!

FATHER *approaches her, hand raised.* MARGOT *snatches up the carving knife and points it at* FATHER.

MARGOT: Keep your hands to yourself! I've had enough of this! I've had it up to here!

MOTHER: Margot, put the knife down.

MARGOT: God damn it! Mamma and Thomas needn't be afraid of God, because they are good. You are not good. And don't think I wouldn't dare. I'm like you. I'm not good either.

FATHER: This family is doomed. The times have poisoned you. Let us pray.

He falls to his knees.

MARGOT: I don't give a damn what you believe. But there'll be no more hitting! You know it's wrong, but you do it anyway. As long as the neighbours don't notice. As long as the rest of the family doesn't know, or the people at the office don't find out. Am I right?

FATHER *struggles to his feet.*

FATHER: I can't stay under the same roof as you. I'm going to sleep in a hotel.

He leaves. MARGOT *puts down the knife and sits at the table, her head in her hands, humming 'Zippity Doo Dah'.*

MOTHER: What have you done, child?

MARGOT: I've finished it.

She bursts into tears.

MOTHER: You've threatened your father with a knife. What will become of us?

MARGOT: Would you rather he kept on beating you? Oh yes, I forgot.

She takes the wooden spoon and breaks it savagely on her knee and goes to throw it.

MOTHER: Not out the window!

MARGOT *throws the wooden spoon out the window.*

THOMAS: Papa was gone for an hour. But then he came back.

FATHER *returns. The family are shocked, but stand together defiantly.*

FATHER: I… have work to do for the office.

He slinks past them, and exits.

Transition scene: THOMAS *practises reading his poem, 'The Guppy'.*

SCENE SIXTEEN

THOMAS, *holding his Ogden Nash book, is in Mrs van Amersfoort's apartment.*

MRS VAN AMERSFOORT: Change of plan, Thomas. We're having the inaugural meeting of the Reading Out Loud Club at your house.

THOMAS: Why?

MRS VAN AMERSFOORT: We thought it would be nicer—your mother and I and your Auntie Pie. Oh, and we're not doing it on Wednesday afternoon.

THOMAS: [*to the audience*] I felt an upset in my tummy, as if I'd swallowed a hippopotamus. [*To* MRS VAN AMERSFOORT] When are we doing it then?

MRS VAN AMERSFOORT: You'll be surprised. Shall I tell you? Here it comes… Tonight.

THOMAS: But what will Pappa say?

MRS VAN AMERSFOORT: Don't be afraid, Thomas. You wanted the plagues of Egypt? Not the frogs, not the flies, not the boils. We're the best plague, we women and children. The pharaoh can't stand against us.

THOMAS: If you say so.

MRS VAN AMERSFOORT: Shut your eyes, Thomas. Take a deep breath and put your hands in your lap.

> THOMAS *does so.*

What do you see?

THOMAS: Nothing... No, wait, I see a desert!

> *Violin music returns.*

MRS VAN AMERSFOORT: And what do you see in that desert?

THOMAS: Sand.

MRS VAN AMERSFOORT: Nothing else?

THOMAS: If I say, you'll think I'm making fun of you.

MRS VAN AMERSFOORT: Just say it.

THOMAS: I see Jesus. Do you mind?

MRS VAN AMERSFOORT: Worse things happen at sea.

> JESUS *appears.*

THOMAS: Jesus always talks to me.

> *He waves to* JESUS, *who waves back.*

MRS VAN AMERSFOORT: And is that good or not so good? If you like we can get rid of him.

THOMAS: I don't mind. Jesus is all alone, you know. I don't think he's got anyone else to talk to.

MRS VAN AMERSFOORT: How sad.

> JESUS *gestures, as if whispering.*

What's he saying now?

THOMAS: That he's coming to the Reading Out Loud Club.

MRS VAN AMERSFOORT: The more the merrier. Thomas, open your eyes.

> THOMAS *does so.*

Are you afraid?

THOMAS: No. Not too much.

MOTHER *calls, causing a snap into the following scene…*

SCENE SEVENTEEN

MOTHER: Thomas, put the extra chairs out. Margot, hurry and do those dishes.

> MOTHER, MARGOT *and* THOMAS *run around organising the room for the Reading Out Loud Club.* FATHER *enters.*

FATHER: What's going on?

MOTHER: We have guests coming. Hurry.

FATHER: What guests?

MARGOT: Auntie Pie…

MOTHER: I still have to get dressed.

FATHER: Just for Auntie Pie?

MOTHER: Of course not, there are lots of other people coming. Maybe you can push the table aside and put the chairs in a circle, Thomas.

FATHER: Who's coming? Why do I only hear about it now?

MARGOT: [*drying the carving knife*] Sorry, Pap. We forgot.

MOTHER: It just went right out of my head.

THOMAS: I wanted to tell you, Pappa, but I went to the toilet… and I forgot.

MOTHER: More chairs, Thomas!

THOMAS: How many do we need?

MOTHER: Auntie Magda's coming too, Auntie Bea, Mrs van Amersfoort, Margot's friends…

MARGOT: … Eliza.

MOTHER: About twelve, I think.

FATHER: Twelve?

MARGOT: She's just saying that. It could be much more.

THOMAS: It's the Reading Out Loud Club—we're doing it every week from now on.

MOTHER: Help Margot with the washing-up, Thomas. I really do have to get dressed now.

> MOTHER *leaves.*

FATHER: Twelve people?

> *Offstage,* MOTHER *sings from 'Zippity Doo Dah'.*

And what about me? What am I supposed to do this evening?

MOTHER: [*off*] Will someone put the coffee on?

MARGOT: I will.

> *The doorbell rings.* THOMAS *opens it and* ELIZA *enters. She is wearing the same dress she wore in Thomas's vision of her in the castle.*

ELIZA: Hello?

> *Silence in the room, except for the creak of her leather leg.* FATHER *stares.*

Hey, Mr Klopper, it's just a leather leg.

> *She pulls up her skirt to show it.* MARGOT *returns.*

MARGOT: Hi, Eliza. Take a seat.

ELIZA: I want to sit next to Thomas, because he's my boyfriend.

> *The violin music starts.* ELIZA *takes* THOMAS*'s hand.*

And, how do I look?

THOMAS: Beautiful! Eliza, does your father play the violin?

ELIZA: How do you know that?

THOMAS: And your mother can sing really beautifully.

ELIZA: You're a very special boy, you know.

THOMAS: A bit, maybe.

> *The doorbell rings.* MARGOT *goes to the door and admits* AUNTIE PIE.

MARGOT: Hey, Auntie Pie! Come in.

AUNTIE PIE: I brought some people with me.

> *She brings a few people from the audience into the space and seats them, inventing names for them as she goes.*

Auntie Magda and Auntie Bea, little Hans and Tineke... and Marleen, Juliet and Anita. Come in, one and all!

MOTHER: [*off*] Leave the front door open. Everybody's welcome!

> AUNTIE PIE *spots* FATHER *and goes to kiss him.*

AUNTIE PIE: Hey there, Man of God? Hey, how do you like my slacks?

> *She shows them off with a bottom wiggle.*

> MRS VAN AMERSFOORT *enters with her gramophone.*

MRS VAN AMERSFOORT: You can get away with that, Pie. My bottom's too big for slacks. Hi, Thomas, how are you feeling?

THOMAS: Fine.

AUNTIE PIE: I hear Thomas is a great reader now. Have you thought about what you want to be when you grow up, Thomas?

THOMAS: Happy. I want to be happy.

FATHER: Only good-for-nothings and fools are happy, Thomas. Give Auntie Pie a proper answer.

THOMAS: [*to* AUNTIE PIE] I want to be happy and that's all.

AUNTIE PIE: A very proper answer if you ask me.

> MOTHER *appears. She wears a light yellow dress, her hair hangs loose and she has lipstick on. She looks beautiful.*

MOTHER: Is everyone alright for coffee?

MRS VAN AMERSFOORT: Wow! Don't you look gorgeous, Mrs Klopper!

> MRS VAN AMERSFOORT *consults her program.*

While we're waiting for everyone to arrive—music! A record from Eliza.

> *She puts the record on the gramophone and Louis Armstrong's trumpet blares out.*

ELIZA: Louis Armstrong!

MOTHER: I love Louis Armstrong!

ELIZA: I've got two more of his records. I'll bring them to Reading Club next week.

> THOMAS *picks up the record sleeve.*

THOMAS: Is this jazz music? I've never seen real live jazz music.

ELIZA: There's so much in the world that we haven't seen. I've never seen a real live Rolls Royce.

MRS VAN AMERSFOORT: Damned good music too, Eliza. It gives me the shivers.

AUNTIE PIE: Where?

> MRS VAN AMERSFOORT *gets up and shimmies provocatively, playfully.*

MRS VAN AMERSFOORT: All over!

> *She and* AUNTIE PIE *dance wildly together as all clap and laugh.*

FATHER *turns the record off.*

FATHER: That's enough of this. I have no interest in listening to any heathen negro music and to stupid empty words. This is my house and... in my house...

MARGOT *stands in front of him, challenging him, humming 'Zippity Doo Dah'.*

She poises the needle over the record again, daring him to stop her.

THOMAS: [*to the audience*] Margot's eyes turned to mirrors. Pappa looked into them and saw himself. Margot was no longer afraid, and before my eyes, I saw her become a witch. But I also saw that Pappa loved her. And that he loved me too, and Mamma...

FATHER *starts to leave, but stops when* MRS VAN AMERSFOORT *announces...*

MRS VAN AMERSFOORT: Reading Out Loud Club item number one will be Thomas reading a verse by Ogden Nash.

THOMAS *prepares to read.* FATHER *waits uncomfortably.* MOTHER *makes a seat ready for him.*

MOTHER: [*to* FATHER] Come on, Abel. Come and sit with us, love.

FATHER *hesitates. He wants to join them, but he wants to get away too. Silence. Everybody is watching him.*

MRS VAN AMERSFOORT: That man is scared. He's scared of... people having fun. He's scared someone will say men evolved from apes. Or that the earth is much more than four thousand years old. Or that someone will ask where Noah got his polar bears from. He's dying on the inside.

MOTHER: [*to* FATHER] Come on, Abel. Come and sit with us. Thomas is going to read.

FATHER *pushes past her and leaves the room.*

FATHER: I can't. I've got work to do for the office.

He goes to his office area, where he falls to his knees, eyes shut in prayer. THOMAS *looks across to him.*

THOMAS: [*to the audience*] I felt as if I had swallowed a hippopotamus, and just after that, I realised that what I felt was pity. I hope that one day, Pappa can sit thinking… by the open window. Not on his knees with his eyes shut.

JESUS *appears.*

Jesus? Can you help Pappa?

JESUS: I'm afraid not.

THOMAS: Do you think Eliza will wait for me?

JESUS: I think so.

THOMAS: Is it scary when she takes off her leather leg?

JESUS: Worse things happen at sea.

THOMAS: I'm going to marry her, you know.

JESUS: You have my blessing.

THOMAS: In my life I have already seen many things. Some of them frightened me. The Bumbiter, a wooden spoon, a swollen nose, a carving knife, Grandpa's false teeth. But some of the things I have seen were beautiful too. One day I'm going to be happy.

He reads 'The Guppy' by Ogden Nash.

JESUS: Thomas will be alright. I could take him into heaven any time, and the angels would be pleased. They all love Thomas. But he wouldn't be interested in my angels. They are all very beautiful, but well… none of them has a leather leg that creaks when they walk. You can't have everything.

THOMAS *finishes his reading, then adds…*

THOMAS: It doesn't mean anything. It's just fun.

MOTHER *leads the applause; then she is joined by the other Reading Out Loud Club guests.* THOMAS *bows.*

LOUIS ARMSTRONG *blares out music for a curtain call.*

THE END